Living and Loving Life One Day at a Time

366 axioms -for every day of the year- to make you think, help get you through every day, and inspire you to live life to the fullest

By
Violette L. Meier

VIORI
PUBLISHING

Viori Publishing
vioripublishing.com
Atlanta, GA

Copyright ©2016 by Violette L. Meier

ISBN: 978-0-9913432-3-2

Printed in the United States of America

Cover Design by Viori Publishing

Dedicated to:

...the wise women of my family: Mommy (Roberta), great-grandmother Mama Sadie, and Auntie Roofie (Johnie Ruth). Through the womb of creation, great wisdom flows into the world. Know that I listen to you, admire you, and have become a better person by knowing you.

Acknowledgements

Special thanks to my husband Ari Meier who is always my biggest supporter. You help me in every way. Thank you for being the epitome of a great man.

Xoe, Zahyir, and Ruah, you are the reason why I began to search for spiritual purity, emotional stability, perceptual balance, and serenity in my life. My goal is always to be a better mother and example for you all. At times I may fall short, but know that I am forever striving.

Other Books by Violette L. Meier:

Violette Ardor: A Volume of Poetry

Out of Night: The First Chronicle of Zayashariya

Angel Crush

Son of the Rock
(Sequel to Angel Crush)

Tales of a Numinous Nature: A Short Story Collection

*This Sickness We Call Love: Poems of Love, Lust, &
Lamentation*

Ruah the Immortal

Living and Loving Life One Day at A Time

Day 1. Love hard and live free.

Day 2. Gratitude is the key to appreciating each moment of every day.

Day 3. Time is one of God's greatest gifts. It puts the worst things far behind us, and gives us opportunity for the best things now.

Day 4. Decide to be happy and you will be.

Day 5. All we have is right now. Live right now. Be happy right now. Forgive right now. Follow your dreams right now. Advocate right now. Protest right now.

Day 6. All of us must face death someday. Today is not that day, so live!

Day 7.   We always prioritize mental health, physical health, financial health, relationship health, and emotional health, but we fail to prioritize spiritual health. Know that your soul is eternal. The rest will fade away. Take care of your spirit first, and everything else will fall into place.

Day 8.   It takes way more effort to be unhappy than to be happy; to hold grudges than to forgive; to worry than to trust.

Day 9.   We must teach our daughters that they are wise, beautiful, and talented. Let them know that they are the zenith of God's creation. Ensure them that everything they need can be found within themselves.

Day 10.   We must explain to our sons that they are virile, powerful, intelligent beings. They are the other half of God's divine equation.   Ensure them that they only need to be themselves, and the world will open up to them.

Day 11.   Those who love you will love you. Those who don't won't.

Day 12.   Self-esteem, unity, community, and spiritual direction start at home.

Day 13.   Freedom is worth more than money, fame, respect, or acclaim. An accomplished slave is still a slave.

Day 14.   Trust no person who ignores the social injustices of the world.

Day 15. Seek God even when you feel that God is so distant that God can't be reached. You'll find yourself in the presence of God and everything will be just fine.

Day 16. Purify your heart and fall humbly before the Lord our God. Forgiveness is there. All you have to do is ask.

Day 17. Pray to always truly see yourself. You can't correct what you refuse to see.

Day 18. Adore yourself and delight in yourself. You are an original masterpiece.

Day 19. Self-governance is the hardest and the highest virtue.

Day 20.   Lusting after material things leads to the deterioration of the soul.

Day 21.   Let money be a source of comfort not a source of corruption.

Day 22.   Acknowledging the success of others does not diminish your accomplishments.

Day 23.   Never compare yourself to anyone. We all have unique gifts and talents. Let's celebrate each other. Everything is not a competition.

Day 24.   Ask God to heal our brokenness so that we will not break each other.

Day 25.   Seek God.

Day 26.   You never have to justify your personal beliefs, your culture, your politics, or your God.

Day 27. God is still at work today. Miracles still happen. People are still being transformed. Scripture is still being written in the hearts of all of God's people.

Day 28. The limited can't limit the limitless.

Day 29. Sex is a form of worship, so don't allow demons to defile your holy temple.

Day 30. We cannot afford to dabble in ignorance, wallow in foolery, or be content with dehumanization.

Day 31. Knowledge is power. Use your power. Share your power.

Day 32. Love transcends religion, gender, culture, nationality, race, sexuality, social position, economic status, and personal opinions.

Day 33. Life is consecrated. Have reverence for life.

Day 34. Never allow people to bind and trap you in their personal beliefs and doctrines. Get to know God for yourself and let the spirit lead you.

Day 35. Infidelity is childish, disrespectful, shows insecurity, and lack of integrity. Being trustworthy is part of being a responsible adult.

Day 36. Protest where it counts, with our money. Economic power is the strongest power in America. If we want change, we must hold on to our change.

Day 37. People are what they do, not what they say.

Day 38. It doesn't take long for a person to show you who they really are. It is up to you to see it.

Day 39. It is impossible for everyone around you to have a problem with you, and you have no responsibility for that problem.

Day 40. One of the reasons people suffer from depression, anxiety, stress, insecurity, and failure is because we allow our thoughts, happiness, and personal image to be defined by advertisers and the media. Why are we trying to meet the expectations of people who are trying to sell us something? If we don't have a deficit, they can't profit.

Day 41. No matter how smart, attractive, wealthy, accomplished, funny, or enlightened you are, some people will never care about you, acknowledge you, or like you. Be at peace with that.

Day 42. Love is everything. Without it, we are nothing.

Day 43. You were made in the image of God. Strut!

Day 44. The more you read, research, and converse; you will realize that we're all making guesses hoping to make sense of our existence.

Day 45. Every day, do a little dance. It's the small things that give joy.

Day 46. It's very important for people to know that you love and are committed to your spouse, and that there is no room for extra people in your relationship. Keep love alive and families together.

Day 47. Temptation only has the power that you give it.

Day 48. When you get an urge to judge, look in the mirror first.

Day 49. Unproductivity is slow suicide.

Day 50. Poetry is in every breath.

Day 51. Let your words be honey sweet, intellectual, powerful, spiritual, motivational, invigorating, and prophetic.

Day 52. You can't confine a supernatural God within your natural logic.

Day 53. Feel the whole of yourself and know in your heart that you are a part of something indivisible, indestructible, terrific, and powerful.

Day 54. Be an oracle of your own life. See visions of grand success by the creativity of your mind and the work of your hands.

Day 55. The sky is a canvas and a new painting is waiting for you each sunset.

Day 56. People hear and see what they want. The truth rarely matters.

Day 57. Being yourself is liberating.

Day 58. Just because someone doesn't agree with you, doesn't mean that they hate you. We all have the right to express our feelings.

Day 59. If you desire true knowledge, you have to learn from a variety of sources and know that all sources have agendas. Consider every perspective then draw your own conclusion.

Day 60. Our children are our most precious resource. We must protect them at all cost.

Day 61. Love is the only thing that will heal the world. Not like. Not lust. Not luxury. Only love. Love is God. God is love.

Day 62. Innocence is beautiful.

Day 63. When an artist dies, the soul weeps.

Day 64. Some people have no interest in knowing who you really are. They are more interested in the person they want you to be.

Day 65. A preacher who is preaching Jesus and doesn't preach social justice isn't preaching Jesus.

Day 66. Never stop pushing, striving, hoping, dreaming, and claiming victory over your life.

Day 67. Learn to let go of people who are hindering forces in your life.

Day 68. Let love infiltrate every aspect of your life by surrounding yourself with people that make every day a pleasure to wake up to.

Day 69. Someone who loves you will tell you the truth when it hurts, tell you when you're wrong, and will refuse to do something that they know is bad for you.

Day 70. Never take for granted that someone loves you.

Day 71. Want to do something radical, exciting, and controversial? Shop in and support your own community.

Day 72. It is wonderful to have pride in who we are, but make no mistake, God is not a racist, a sexist, an economic elitist, or a hater of any human being. God created us all in His/Her/Its image.

Day 73. Romance isn't dead. It is just put to sleep by impatience, lust, and lack of communication.

Day 74. As flawed creatures, it is only fair to judge each other with compassion and understanding.

Day 75. Don't allow emotions to take you to places you can't escape.

Day 76. Loving yourself is the best way to teach children to love themselves.

Day 77. Don't allow yourself to become a slave to anything. Master your weaknesses before they master you.

Day 78. Relationships with people help define who we are.

Day 79. It's not enough to love your mate. You have to like them too.

Day 80. If you can learn to be happy regardless of your situation, you can make it through any trial or tribulation.

Day 81. Surround yourself with godly people and watch divine things happen in your life.

Day 82. Cultivate your mind and become circumcised of heart.

Day 83. A close family is the greatest blessing a person can have.

Day 84. You can make only so much money, drink so much alcohol, have so much sex, and eat so much food before you realize that nothing will fill the void but God.

Day 85. It's okay to be a square in a world of circles.

Day 86. The goal is to have someone who will still love you when beauty fades, if money gets low, and age takes a toll.

Day 87. We are all complex characters, walking contradictions, oceans of secrets; people of many layers.

Day 88. Don't allow others to define who you are. That is your assignment in life.

Day 89. Be kind to everyone you encounter. You never know how you will impact others and how they may impact you.

Day 90. The most beautiful woman is the room is the one who likes herself the most.

Day 91. It is not God's will that anyone be a willful idiot. Make no mistake, knowledge is power and we are supposed to be powerful forces in the world.

Day 92. The only thing new under the sun is you.

Day 93.   Smile. You have plenty to smile about.

Day 94.   There is absolutely no honor in stupidity.

Day 95.   Do better.

Day 96.   Just because a person is in a bad situation, doesn't mean that they can't offer good advice. Sometimes they are a real life example of a cautionary tale.

Day 97.   The only person you can govern is yourself.

Day 98.   Laugh every day. There is always something that will bring delight.

Day 99.   Having a sense of humor is a prerequisite for happiness.

Day 100.   Happy thoughts create a happy reality.

Day 101. Taking responsibility for yourself is the first step in becoming an enlightened person.

Day 102. Your dream is never impossible to obtain. It all depends on how badly you want to obtain it.

Day 103. If you don't want a better life, you won't get a better life.

Day 104. Helping others heals us.

Day 105. Have faith or worry. Doing both is impossible because faith eliminates the need to worry and worrying reveals that you have no faith.

Day 106. Most times, our circumstance is the direct result of our choices.

Day 107. Fall in love, laugh, dance, travel, praise, give! Life is for living, so live!

Day 108.   Life is poetry.

Day 109.   We are a part of something supernatural. There has to be something inside this physical form that holds the emotional galaxy of our being.

Day 110.   There is no such thing as unconditional devotion. Cause and effect determine the yearnings of the heart.

Day 111.   Every viewpoint is valuable, but if what you share is purposely deceptive, is cruel and offensive, seeks to destroy others or yourself, is inhumane, promotes degenerate behavior, seeks to dumb down not to enlighten or is aiding in the breakdown of the community at large, WHAT YOU ARE SPEWING IS STUPIDITY!

Day 112. A woman is the womb of creation, bearer of life, carrier of civilizations, the essence of beauty, love personified, intelligence amplified, poetry realized, and perfection finalized.

Day 113. Those who harm children are the worst among humanity.

Day 114. A man is the protector of nations, alternate image of the divine, strength magnified, potent life, father of knowledge, world builders, spiritual guide, and king of queen.

Day 115. Science and God complement one another not eliminate one another.

Day 116. Evil can pour over into a good life and leave destruction in its wake. Good can bring light into a life of darkness and change the path of the hopeless to the hopeful. Our actions matter. Our words matter. Our thoughts matter. If we want our world to be a better place, we have to become better people.

Day 117. God did not make us to torture us. Every temptation, struggle, or weakness we have can be overcome. We are not deficient creatures. We are beautifully and wonderfully made; mini-gods created in the image of God!

Day 118. The fruit of our faith should be nourishment to all around us.

Day 119. Leave the judging to God and only offer meaningful correction.

Day 120. True repentance and transformation is the way to conquer the things that make us weak.

Day 121. When we are able to face the mirror and see our true imperfections, this is when God gives us the ability to do better.

Day 122. Sex is a smoldering fire that must be contained within the confines of a committed relationship. If it burns free, it will burn down your whole life. If it is suffocated, the flame will die, leaving you cold and callous. Keep it in its proper place and your heart and bed will be warm for a lifetime.

Day 123. Life has a way of humbling us if we refuse to humble ourselves.

Day 124.   Have no fear of the mortal but of The Great Immortal!

Day 125.   Help transform the world by actions not just words.

Day 126.   Declutter your life by getting rid of things that have no purpose in making your life better.

Day 127.   Generosity is a blessing to the giver and the receiver.

Day 128.   Celebrate beauty in everything, and beauty will be celebrated in you. A critical eye reflects your own ugliness.

Day 129.   Say I love you as often as you can. You never know when the opportunity will be taken away.

Day 130.   Passive aggressiveness is the shroud of the fearful.

Day 131.   Enabling people, wounds to the point of debilitation.

Day 132.   Never be afraid to ask for what you want. The worst someone can say is no. If that no is final, move on to something or someone who will give you your yes.

Day 133.   Have a charitable heart at all times. You have no idea how your generosity can improve someone's perspective of the world.

Day 134.   Getting lost in imaginary assumptions can cause you to lose real life relationships.

Day 135.   Don't be so quick to think the worst of someone. Their goodness may sincerely surprise you.

Day 136. A perfect ménage a trois is between you, your family, and your life's work.

Day 137. Words are like magic. They can make things manifest right before your eyes; so, speak beauty, joy, and peace instead of ugliness, depression, and strife.

Day 138. The truth can be hard to listen to, but we must listen anyway. Although each word may cut, they also mend and make us better.

Day 139. Use every available opportunity to learn something new. New knowledge makes the brain happy.

Day 140. A life of service to others is a life lived excellently because the circle of helping and giving is perpetual. As you pour out blessings, blessings are poured upon you.

Day 141. Be merciful beings full of compassion and understanding for one day you will require some measure of mercy from others.

Day 142. When you decide to be happy, nothing or no one can change that. Joy becomes an innate part of your biology.

Day 143. My great grandmother always said, "If someone isn't treating you right, drop them out of your pocket like a piece of lint."

Day 144. Sit at the feet of the wise and try to capture everything that falls from their lap.

Day 145. If you feel that you are the most intelligent person you know, you need to get to know more people.

Day 146. Speak your true intentions at all times.

Day 147. It is insanity to follow every lust and desire because it is impossible to fill a bottomless hole. Work on closing the hole, and your obsessions will discontinue.

Day 148. Strive for perfection with the perfect understanding that you will never reach it.

Day 149. Confidence often alters perceptions of beauty.

Day 150. Life is not that serious. Don't overthink things. Stop living in your head and start living in this spectacular world made just for you.

Day 151. Relationships are not meant to be one sided. Participate and demand participation.

Day 152. It's okay to live in a bubble as long as you know it will eventually be popped.

Day 153. Great pain can be avoided by knowing the difference between friends and associates.

Day 154. Resist the desire to retaliate. Nothing will change what has already happened, nor will it make you feel any better. Move on.

Day 155. Stop trying to make things that mean nothing mean something.

Day 156. Believe with your whole heart that you can accomplish every goal that you set for yourself, and you will never be disappointed with the outcome of your efforts.

Day 157. Your gift is the thing that comes most natural to you. Focus on being the best at that, and success will be guaranteed.

Day 158. Reassess your ideas of success. Decide what it means to you. Ignore what others think your success should look like.

Day 159. Religiosity without spirituality is like a sandwich without bread.

Day 160. When a person loves you, honor that love. Real love is rare and seldom found. Learn to distinguish between striking oil and splashing in a muddy puddle.

Day 161. There is nothing sexier than a man who is comfortable in his virility, intelligence, and competence.

Day 162.   Apologize when you are wrong. Don't gloat when you are right. Ask questions when you don't know.

Day 163.   I don't know is a perfectly acceptable answer. Just make sure that you seek to find out.

Day 164.   Holding grudges serve no purpose, but to ensure unhappiness.

Day 165.   Take yourself on a wild adventure at least once a year. We all need great memories to relish when we are old.

Day 166.   Be wary of anyone who can find fault in everyone but themselves.

Day 167.   No one is all bad. No one is all good. We all wallow in the middle somewhere.

Day 168. Be a better person than you were the minute before, the day before, the week before, the year before, and the decade before.

Day 169. Young fools will grow up to be old fools if they refuse to mature.

Day 170. Honor the elderly. They have seen more of the world than you have. There is a strong possibility that they know something that you don't.

Day 171. Do something you have never done before. Life is only as good as your experiences.

Day 172. Don't be afraid to love. Love is an exquisite drama that we all pray to play a part in.

Day 173. Abusing your body is an insult to the Creator.

Day 174. When something is teetering on the edge of addiction, pull back and gain balance. Once you fall over the cliff, there is no telling if you will survive the plunge.

Day 175. Greed and selfishness will alienate you faster than the plague.

Day 176. Go outside and let the sun rays bathe you. There is something about the light that will brighten your attitude.

Day 177. The monster under the bed is fear.

Day 178. Caste out your demons. Refuse to live with them.

Day 179. You can only get so far without God.

Day 180. The goal of sex is not to have sex with as many people as you can, but to have as much sex as you can with the person that you love.

Day 181. Pray until the thunder of the world becomes the whisper of God.

Day 182. Guard your peace for there are those who wish to rob you of it twenty-four hours a day.

Day 183. Stop cloning personalities for yourself. Decide on who you are going to be, and be that person.

Day 184. While roaming through the labyrinth of life, don't fumble around lost and afraid. Admire the greenery. Appreciate the design. Enjoy the walk.

Day 185. Be gentle with the hearts of others. They are just as delicate as yours.

Day 186. Channel your anger into something less destructive like exercise or creativity.

Day 187. Worshipping the preacher instead of the God is like making love with gloved hands; touching but not feeling; comforting but not healing.

Day 188. Being yourself is the greatest gift you can give to anyone.

Day 189. Only children have an endless fascination with their genitals. Adults understand that they are so much more than their sexuality.

Day 190. Being in love with a person and being in love with the idea of a person are two different things.

Living and Loving Life One Day at A Time

Day 191. Sad days will come; so will happy ones. Keep the same positive attitude every day and every day will be a blessed day.

Day 192. Nothing is crueler than being in a relationship with someone you don't love.

Day 193. Tell those whom you love that you love them every chance you can get. It is unknown when the last chance will pass.

Day 194. Walk in faith at all times. Our faith can create or destroy the world we build for ourselves.

Day 195. Always be kind to children, they are the purest aspect of humanity.

Day 196. There is peace in connecting to the earth. Feel the grass between your toes. Let the dirt sift through your fingers. Dance around a tree. Joy will consume you when you let go and love life.

Day 197. Holding a grudge is like willingly walking around with a rock in your shoe.

Day 198. Some people have no interest in changing the world, just complaining about it.

Day 199. Don't forget to be happy.

Day 200. Always be kind to everyone you encounter. You ever know how you may impact a life or how your life may be impacted.

Day 201.   Don't be angry with people for being who they told you they were.

Day 202.   People can't be put in boxes. We're complex characters, walking contradictions, oceans of secrets, people of many layers.

Day 203.   Intelligent people can listen to the opinions of others and still have their own.

Day 204.   Bad boys break your heart. Good men protect it.

Day 205.   Have faith that you are protected, loved, and filled with everything you need to be successful.

Day 206.   Life is a walk on thin ice.

Day 207. Be kind. Don't focus on imperfections, but see the good side of people and yourself. Compliment not criticize.

Day 208. There is no such thing as an utopian society. All we can ever do is live our best and love each other the best way we know how.

Day 209. If you are disenchanted with community leaders, take over the struggle and show them the change you seek. Step up or shut up.

Day 210. Enjoy today; this hour, this moment, this second because you will never experience it again. Carpe Diem! Seize the day!

Day 211. Support the dreams of others. No one can make it alone.

Day 212. As interpreters and doers of God's will and word, it is not our job to judge others. Our job is to bring people to God and let God heal whatever is broken in their lives.

Day 213. Learn to think for yourself and use your own judgment. Don't allow others to form your]opinions.

Day 214. School is not the only place a person can get a superb education. Read, listen, observe, learn, and live.

Day 215. Don't let the hardships of life break you. The human spirit is immortal and invincible. God created you to endure. So endure!

Day 216.   I struggle with faith at times because it means that I have to relinquish control and allow God to take the wheel. Letting go is hard, but when I do, God takes me on the most fantastic rides.

Day 217.   It is important to surround yourself with positive people. Dysfunction begat dysfunction.

Day 218.   Cast away your burdens and dwell on what is beautiful, joyful, positive, and good about your life.

Day 219.   Everyone has a vice. Some are just not as obvious as others. Learn to morph vices into virtues by taking away their power over your life.

Day 220. Surround yourself with people who dream. If you associate with people who have no vision, eventually your sight will become dim.

Day 221. The universe is not The Creator. It is a creation. God and the universe are not synonymous. Know the difference.

Day 222. Look for something positive in everyone you encounter, and you will be surprised how people will see the positive in you.

Day 223. Today, support someone. Be an ear. Try to inspire. Give love. Be a friend. Cheer them on. Listen. The focus should not always be you.

Day 224.   You can't fix someone a cup of crap and tell them it's cranberry juice, and then be mad when they won't drink it. Present your best, and you will get the best response.

Day 225.   Congratulate yourself for every success no matter how large or small.

Day 226.   Not only set high goals, but also enjoy the progression to the top.

Day 227.   Never ever stop believing that true love is real.

Day 228.   Allow yourself to be happy. It is a gift that will make every day a miracle.

Day 229.   Go to nature to find peace. God is there. Let the wind speak to your spirit.

Day 230. Life is not as complicated as we pretend.

Day 231. Relationships are the foundation to a joyful existence.

Day 232. I believe in the afterlife but, no one really knows what will happen after death. However, we do know what happens in this life, so we must choose to live the best we can now.

Day 233. Helping others can provide the healing you need.

Day 234. Making lists and setting goals can give you a reason to live even when you don't want to.

Day 235. Know that your self-worth can't be purchased at a store. It has to be hand crafted in your heart and displayed in your actions.

Day 236. Sex is worship at the most extraordinary level.

Day 237. Be honest with yourself at all times and humility will come naturally.

Day 238. Torturing yourself is not the road to divinity.

Day 239. You will be surprised how much God talks if you shut up and listen.

Day 240. The existence of evil is a byproduct of our own freewill.

Living and Loving Life One Day at A Time

Day 241. Evil comes in many forms. One of the ugliest is witnessing evil take place and remaining silent and inactive.

Day 242. Gossip is like a knife tied to a pendulum. Once it starts moving, its cut reaches higher and further than ever imagined.

Day 243. It's okay to let go of people. Everyone isn't meant to be with you through every stage of life.

Day 244. Learning to say no is hard, but it can make life easier.

Day 245. Turn your moments of wonderment into a moment of worship.

Day 246. May the Spirit of God hover over your darkness until there is light.

Day 247. When people tell you an unflattering truth about yourself, don't get defensive, but display gratitude for they are bringing light to a dark place in you.

Day 248. Prayer is the ultimate life changer. It bridges gaps, sews on patches, moisturizes deserts, warms the cold, and makes the impossible possible. Tap into its power and life will never be the same.

Day 249. Being created in the image of the Creator, it is our divine duty to create. Creation is the core of our existence; therefore, our life depends on our productivity.

Day 250. Love teeters between gladness and sadness; rationality and madness; ecstasy and pain; sunbeams and rain.

Day 251. Even the most hedonistic of hearts must find self-control or the fire of desire will burn you to death.

Day 252. Most people are innately good. Tap into that good and see the greater good tap into you.

Day 253. Life isn't always beautiful. Sometimes it is positively grotesque! When ugly times are upon you, don't try to paint them pretty. Stare at the ugly. Learn from it. Wrestle with it, but don't become twisted in it. Gain strength from its monstrous grasp so you can break loose and become more powerful than before.

Day 254. Being unrealistic only leads to constant disappointment.

Day 255. Pretending to be blind to injustice rots the soul.

Day 256. When life scares you, don't hide your wound in shame. but wear it as a badge of courage so that others will marvel at how victoriously you made it through.

Day 257. Perfection is as obtainable as a unicorn with a golden fleece.

Day 258. Education and freedom are soulmates.

Day 259. A person ignorant of their history is like a vagabond with no home, purpose, or foreseeable future.

Living and Loving Life One Day at A Time

Day 260. God reveals miracles every day of our lives. We just have to be open to seeing them.

Day 261. Life is nothing more than a parade of memories that never stop marching.

Day 262. Diet and exercise should be never be neglected. The body is the house of the spirit. If that house fails, you spirit must transcend from this life. Transcendence before its time is a tragedy.

Day 263. A compliment can save a life.

Day 264. It doesn't take an eon to figure out if you love someone.

Day 265. The human mind has the ability to adjust to anything. Be careful about what you allow yourself to adjust to.

Day 266. Never be afraid to ask for what you want. No is the worst thing you can hear, and once you hear no, just go on and ask someone else. Yes will eventually come even if you have to make yes happen on your own volition.

Day 267. Being silly sometimes is a youth regenerator.

Day 268. Like yourself. Love yourself. Loathe yourself. Whatever you feel, others will too!

Day 269. Beauty is what you think it is.

Day 270. You can't control what people think of you, but you can control what you think of yourself.

Day 271. Give away 99% of your heart. Hold on to 1%. That is where sanity lives.

Day 272. When you accept that people are just as flawed and multi-layered as you are, you will never be disappointed.

Day 273. Be responsible for your own emotions. No one can control the roller coaster in your head.

Day 274. Trying to convince an idiot of anything is like trying to teach a fish to walk.

Day 275. Feel compassion for unhappy people. They have to wake up every day to themselves.

Day 276. Be kind to everyone you meet because you may be unknowingly speaking with the divine.

Day 277. Always leave room for the supernatural to explain what the natural cannot.

Day 278. Words have destroyed more hearts than cardiac arrest.

Day 279. If acknowledging the suffering and mistreatment of others offends you, there is an excellent chance that you are the villain in their nightmare.

Day 280. Don't allow your pride to take away all that you hold dear. Pride's main purpose is to destroy your relationships and leave you destitute.

Day 281. Force yourself to believe in yourself. Be confident to the edge of delusion!

Day 282. Our souls animating our bodies; pure poetry. Life!

Day 283. The vigorous thrusting pulse of life is enough to breath poetry.

Day 284. Boredom and laziness are slave masters with fuzzy shackles.

Day 285. Stop dreaming and your life will become a nightmare.

Day 286. Being sexy is as simple as loving who you are, just how you are.

Day 287. A person trying to navigate life without God is like a mathematician who forgets how to count.

Day 288. "I don't know" is a suitable answer if it is the truth.

Day 289. True love between a man and a woman is the closest thing humans will ever get to heaven on earth.

Day 290. When the urge to judge someone harshly comes upon you, take a moment to review some of the not so good choices you have made in your life.

Day 291. Life is way too precious to waste being angry, reminiscing on the past, or stewing in disappointment. Enjoy your days for they are numbered, and you have no idea what number you're on.

Day 292. Talents are God's way of telling us I love you.

Day 293. Be generous with your smile, your kindness, your gratitude, your possessions, and your spirituality.

Day 294. No one is a victim of everyone and everything all the time. After a while, you become a victim of yourself. Stop offering your neck to be stepped on.

Day 295. Want to be original? Practice being a good person. It's easier to make bad choices than good choices. It takes power to stay positive.

Day 296. Shun knowledge. Lose power.

Day 297. A person who continually judges must avoid mirrors at all times.

Day 298. Sometimes pain is cleansing. Afterwards, our old self is shed and our new improved selves emerge from the excruciating sludge.

Day 299. Be still and wait on God and you will be renewed. Patience and faith will birth your revival.

Day 300. Reminiscing on past incidents or mentally reenacting memories is a waste of precious life.

Day 301.   Living in the past is like sitting at a table full of food and starving to death because you refuse to see what's in front of you.

Day 302.   Loving someone who doesn't love you back is a slow and grueling suicide attempt.

Day 303.   Fear is the number one cause of dream death.

Day 304.   When you finally figure out that the only thing you can control in life is yourself, life will become a lot less complicated.

Day 305.   The intricate working of the universe and the life that dwells within it is ample enough evidence that God exists.

Day 306. Being fearless and being stupid are two different things. Fearlessness means to walk in faith and confidence. Being stupid means to walk into anything, anyway, at any time.

Day 307. Don't fill the hole in your heart with things that are going to make it bigger.

Day 308. Fantasizing about the past will only blind you to the present.

Day 309. Allow yourself to love fully and freely. May your heart overflow from every sensation birthed by love's liberation.

Day 310. Beauty is much more than the way you look. It is how you carry yourself. The way you move. The light that shines from you. Pure confidence and humanity intertwined. It is an inner radiance that draws the eye to you.

Day 311. Learn not to waste your time on people who will never give you what you need or want.

Day 312. If you are a witness to evil and do nothing, you are a working component of that evil.

Day 313. Set personal goals daily so that you are constantly reminded of your accomplishments. Often times, we forget that we are achievers.

Day 314. Get lost in kisses every chance you get.

Day 315. Love is the cornerstone of positivity. It allows us to feel good and make others feel good. It is divine reciprocity.

Day 316. A person who never learns from their experiences is like a thirsty person with a cup of water, but forgetting to drink it.

Day 317. Work daily to destroy stereotypes and biases. They are only distractions blinding you to the fact that people are all the same.

Day 318. Memories are deceitful creatures that trick you into making a mistake twice.

Day 319. Nothing is as bad as it could be.

Day 320. Sharing your skills and gifts with a younger generation guarantees that innovation, imagination, and invention will always endow greater opportunities.

Day 321. Jobs, money, projects, movements, religions, social clubs, or the like should ever take precedence over family. Home should be the place where your impact should be the most relevant. Why save the world if your world will be destroyed?

Day 322. Don't be with someone who is just attracted to your physical beauty, but be with someone who adores the intricate workings of your cerebral artistry. The mind will last when beauty takes its last bow.

Day 323. The world is big enough for all of us to have a bit of happiness.

Day 324. We're all famous to the people who love us.

Day 325. Be sensitive to the viewpoints of others, but understand that their perspectives are just their perspectives. We are all responsible for our own truths, and our truths must never be overshadowed by the truths of others.

Day 326. You can't teeter between salvation and damnation daily; praying with your fingers crossed. Have faith or have no faith at all. The choice is yours.

Day 327. When you swallow and digest pain, it will only fill you with hurt. Learn to vomit up those things that seek to destroy you and flush them down the toilet.

Day 328. Tolerating hard-to-deal-with people is an art that is not praised nearly enough.

Day 329. Take and give compliments as freely as breathing.

Day 330. One can be spiritual without being religious or religious without being spiritual. The key is to seek balance between both worlds so the natural and supernatural can thrive in seamless unity.

Day 331. Everyone needs someone to take care of them, but when we enable people, it stunts their growth and hinders them from reaching their full potential which will, in the long run, cripple them to a point of no rehabilitation.

Day 332. There is nothing poetic about a senseless death.

Day 333. Live fancy free for you and me.

Day 334. Relish getting older because when you stop, you're dead.

Day 335. Look in the mirror and admire the personal uniqueness you possess. Appreciate your skin tone, your facial features, your hair texture, your body, and your style. Get comfortable loving and liking yourself.

Day 336. Men and women are different. That's what makes us awesome. Celebrate those differences. There are strengths in both sexes. Embrace who you are.

Day 337. Don't allow the opinion of others to destroy the purpose you were meant to fulfill. Do what was put in your heart to do. No one can change your destiny but you!

Day 338. A good sense of humor makes life a lot less stressful. If you look hard enough, there is something funny in every situation.

Day 339. There is nothing wrong with laughing to keep from crying. There are enough tears drowning the world.

Day 340. Wisdom is knowing that you only know the smallest amount of what there is to know.

Day 341. The aim of human relations is to not be blind to color, but to see color, admire the diversity of it, and fall in love with the similarities and the differences of each splendid hue.

Day 342. Cultural superiority and inferiority are constructs of a demented imagination.

Day 343. Pieces of broken hearts build towers that house abandoned dreams.

Day 344. One can never receive too many butterfly kisses.

Day 345. Some say the great die young. I say the greatest die old enough to teach the following generations the legend of those who perished.

Day 346. Odd people make humankind so much more fascinating.

Day 347. Artist, oddballs, poets, drama queens, writers, and mystics are pops of color in a beige world.

Day 348. Failure and success are conjoined twins.

Day 349. What matters most is what you want to matter most.

Day 350. You can't expect epic outcomes with basic efforts.

Day 351.   There are so many wondrous ways that you can celebrate life. The most wondrous of them all is being yourself.

Day 352.   Be lust drunk on life. There is no greater high than being a conscious soul in tuned with existence.

Day 353.   Nothing feels better than meeting a goal or seeing a dream realized. It must be like when God said, "Let there be light," and it was.

Day 354.   People who have no dreams or live unproductive lives are destined to become emotional vampires who suck the joy out of everyone they encounter.

Day 355.   Stop worrying about how things are supposed to be. Accept how it is, then change it to what you want it to be.

Violette L. Meier

Day 356. People underestimate the power of shaking one's booty to a great song. Each hip movement shakes off negativity and each thrust welcome positive vibes. Let loose and enjoy yourself sometimes.

Day 357. The people you surround yourself with are the people you become.

Day 358. It only takes a small amount of time before cracks appear in masks.

Day 359. Heroes are the people who speak up when no one else will, shield the weak and humble the strong, refuse to be encumbered by fear, live their lives without apology, and groove to their own rhythm.

Day 360. The sickness we call love is a sickness I hope never finds a cure.

Day 361. Never consider wasting a moment of your life with someone who feels that they are settling for that moment.

Day 362. People who are brave enough to live their lives outside the box, over the limits, beyond the borders, are people who you want surrounding you and pushing you to do the same.

Day 363. Hate and stupidity cannot be confined within race, culture, or politics. It is the mantra of the intellectual dregs of society, representing the worst of humanity.

Day 364. No person is more dangerous than one who has a dream and faith in that dream. There is no stopping the creative force that will launch that dream into reality.

Day 365.   Grab hold to the fullness of life and squeeze out every drop; for it is a miracle to simply exist, to witness the world through your eyes.

Day 366.   The inspiration of God has been revealed through many different belief systems. We all must find our own philosophy or a mentor to follow. Yeshua (Jesus) is my role model, my favorite person, my spiritual teacher, the cornerstone of my life because his teachings are simple: love God, love people, don't judge, and forgiveness. Everything falls under that umbrella. You can't love God without loving people. You can't love people if you constantly stand in judgment. Forgiveness is needed from God and people to continue in love. It's the cycle of divinity. Yeshua forces us to live life looking in the mirror first, and then looking around us.